Diana, The Princess of Wales

Hugh Montgomery-Massingberd's other books
include *The Monarchy*, *The British Aristocracy*,
The Ritz and *The Country Life Book of Royal Palaces
Castles and Homes*. Born in 1946 and educated at
Harrow, he gave up his place reading history at
Cambridge in 1968 to work for Burke's
publications, with which he has been associated
ever since. The numerous Burke's volumes he
has edited include *The Royal Family*, *Landed
Gentry*, *Presidential Families of USA*, *Irish Family
Records*, *Royal Families of the World* and *Country
Houses*. He contributes to various newspapers
and periodicals; he broadcasts and lectures
frequently on royalty and social history.

Diana
The Princess of Wales
Hugh Montgomery-Massingberd

Fontana Paperbacks

Created and produced by Robert Dudley and John Stidolph
Antler Books Ltd, 24–26 Blackfriars Lane, London EC4

Designed by Bill Chouffot

First published by Fontana Paperbacks 1982
Copyright © Antler Books 1982
ISBN 0 00 636538 8

Set in Palatino

Made and printed in Great Britain by
Fakenham Press Limited, Fakenham, Norfolk

Contents

The Love that Pays the Price

To be born to succeed to the throne, as the Prince of Wales was, is one thing; to choose to become the Princess of Wales, and then ultimately Queen, is quite another. That is what Lady Diana Spencer did when she decided at the age of only nineteen to marry Prince Charles. One can hardly overestimate the personal sacrifices involved in dedicating her life to the cause of constitutional monarchy and the never-ending duties it entails.

The character and background of the new third lady of the land have been widely likened to those of the second lady, the Queen Mother, and the comparison is a valid one in many ways. Certainly these two far from cold daughters of earls have been the best things to happen to the Royal Family this century. When considering the extent of the Princess of Wales's commitment, though, it is worth remembering that the Queen Mother turned the Duke of York down at first for fear of royal public life and at that stage there was no reason to believe he would ever become King. "Even today," observed the Queen Mother's biographer, Elizabeth Longford, "a twenty-year-old girl might hesitate before dipping her toe into the magical dew-pond of royal life. It would be lovely to dance in a fairy-ring for ever, with no chores, no traffic jams, no queues. Looked at from the inside, however, that magic circle might seem more like a noose: unremitting public service of a specially repetitive and conventional kind, from which there was no escape." That was written shortly before the Queen Mother's grandson proposed to Lady Diana, giving her time to think it over.

In the event, she did not hesitate to put her head in that "noose"; her affirmative came "quite promptly". First and foremost she was ("of course") in love with him – gossips would have one believe that she had nurtured a crush on the Prince even before their 'first' (according to the authorized version) meeting in a ploughed field, out shooting in 1977. But it would be quite wrong to regard the full significance of the decision as being unappreciated by a giggly, star-struck teenager.

This initial image, projected remorselessly by the media, should not colour people's understanding of the Princess. What modest, tall girl of nineteen wouldn't appear gawky, gauche, coltish,

and so forth, when suddenly subjected to such a phenomenal glare? The silly notion of 'Shy Di' – and how she disliked that diminutive – sold her short. In reality, she has a quiet self-confidence and an engagingly natural manner.

Clues as to her character were not easy to spot amidst the gallons of gush and tons of trivia that are always churned out on these occasions. The trouble with this spillage of 'royal oil' is that (like the man crying 'wolf') when someone such as Lady Diana Spencer comes along who really deserves the works, the awful old clichés – radiant, fairy-tale, enchanting, etc – sound quite inadequate. Happily, the pictures told more of the story. Even the most hardened cynic capitulated to her charm; apart from admiring her beauty, men seemed to feel protective towards her – everyone was agreed that here was an exceptionally lovely girl. As her school-friend and flat-mate Carolyn Pride pointed out: "It wouldn't do any good if she looked like the back-end of a bus."

We were soon regaled with such items as that Lady Diana liked ABBA as well as opera, tap-dancing, animals, baked beans and ballet, ski-ing and swimming; and that she was a conscientious performer of household chores in her flat in Coleherne Court. "I love her sense of humour," said Carolyn Pride. "I love her thoughtfulness and her kind-ness, and the fact that she's a very companionable person. And someone with whom you would never be bored." Lady Diana's sister, Lady Sarah Mc-Corquodale, who brought about that meeting in the ploughed field when her own name was being linked with the Prince, felt the engaged couple would be "totally compatible" in marriage as they had "the same sense of humour; she is very giggly and he is giggly." The Prince himself mentioned music and the outdoors as two particular mutual interests.

Lady Diana felt her "roots" to be in Norfolk ("I have always loved it there"), where she was born on the Sandringham estate, and this emphatically rural environment surely played an important part in the forming of her character. Norfolk is rather a world of its own and the families that live there are notable for producing tweed-clad sirens with a pronounced love of the country, nature and sport, ready to walk long distances besides their partridge-shooting menfolk over heavy land in the teeth of the icy east wind.

Her father, a long-time shooting companion of the Royal Family, the eighth Earl Spencer, who now lives at Althorp, the family seat in Northamptonshire, described his youngest daughter as "a giver, not a taker" and was in no doubt that she would "do the job ahead very well". His former wife, Lady Diana's mother, is now married to Peter Shand Kydd, a farmer; and the latter commented that his step-daughter was "a very genuine person". Lady Diana's step-mother, Raine (daughter of Barbara Cartland, the romantic novelist) was reported as describing her as "sweet and even-tempered". More and more unreliable quotes were beamed across the world as Lady Diana's fascination grew and grew.

Divorce is a hard school and her parents' splitting up when Lady Diana was five must obviously have had a profound effect upon her personality. There is no doubt that she gained an inner strength from the experience, learning a certain toughness, as well as tact and discretion. Alison Miller summed up the royal bride's credentials nicely in the *Sunday Times Magazine*: "serious but not boring; sweet but not *too* sweet; funny, not silly; sporty, not horsey and sexy without being brassy."

Far from being a handicap, her extreme youth turned out to be a positive advantage. For the Princess can be said to have been fortunate in her generation which has tended to mature much earlier than that, say, of her elder sisters. She and her circle of friends seem to be refreshingly old-fashioned and conventional, with good manners and what used to be called a bottom of commonsense, while retaining the proper youthful spirit. They appear to have learnt from their seniors' mistakes, to have dispensed with a lot of the traditional hang-ups. To label this unsung new breed as 'boring' is to misunderstand them; for they have rejected the pomposity and snobbery of their parents' generation just as much as they have turned their backs on the insecure trendiness of the 1960s and its dreary consequences. What is more, they have an extra vitality of their own. In the view of the *Tatler* magazine, girls of this 'born-again generation' choose to play it safe rather than have safety chosen for them. The Princess observed the antics of the older generation and drew her own conclusions

11

Below: The Prince and Princess with Prince Andrew
at Covent Garden for Romeo and Juliet
Opposite: The Palace photo-call, 24 February 1981

about their merits, or otherwise; in short, "She knows what she's missed and doesn't care."

The Prince of Wales, who is over a dozen years her senior, was a fish out of water in the hippy age and picked his friends out of a group some years older than himself. Finding a suitable bride from among his own contemporaries appeared to be a tricky business and the emergence of this new generation whose values are much more akin to his own was a godsend. When it came to the point, the long list of runners in the Prin-

cess of Wales stakes was left standing by the perfect candidate who represented the apotheosis of this new breed.

To grasp the significance of this attractive new generation is to find the key to Lady Diana Spencer's momentous decision to let her love – in the words of her favourite hymn *"I Vow to Thee My Country"* – pay the price. "It wasn't a difficult decision in the end," she said in an interview on the day the engagement was officially announced (24 February 1981). "It was what I wanted – it's what I want."

Court Circles

On 8 June 1961 at her rambling house on the Sandringham estate, Viscountess Althorp watched the royal wedding being broadcast on television from York Minster where her younger daughter, Jane (then aged four) was a bridesmaid to the new Duchess of Kent. Three weeks later, on 1 July, Lady Althorp gave birth at Park House to a third daughter, Diana Frances. Ironically, Diana did not have a royal 'sponsor' (or godparent) whereas the Queen Mother stood sponsor for the eldest sister Sarah; the Duke of Kent for Jane and the Queen herself for brother Charles who was born in 1964. Diana's father, Lord Althorp (who succeeded his father, a godson of Edward VII, in the Spencer earldom in 1975), was a godson of both Queen Mary (the last Princess of Wales) and of her son the Prince of Wales, later Edward VIII.

These links merely hint at the plethora of connections between the present Princess of Wales's family circle and the court. Her maternal grandfather, the fourth Lord Fermoy, who as an Irish peer was able to sit in the House of Commons for King's Lynn, leased Park House from King George V and was a friend of King George VI, with whom he was out shooting hares on the eve of the King's death in 1952. Following his own death three years later, Lord Fermoy's widow Ruth, a keen musician, joined the household of her close friend the Queen Mother. Shortly before Lord Fermoy died, his daughter Frances married Lord

Althorp, son and heir of the seventh Earl Spencer, and the young couple – Diana's mother was only eighteen when she married – later settled at Park House, carrying on the royal lease.

The Princess of Wales's paternal grandmother, the late Countess Spencer, was also a long-standing friend of the Queen Mother and a member of her household, as have been no less than four of her great-aunts – Lady Delia Peel, Lady Annaly, Lady Katharine Seymour and the Dowager Duchess of Abercorn. The Queen Mother was a bridesmaid at Lady Annaly's wedding. The redoubtable Lady Delia who, like Lavinia Annaly, was a sister of the late Lord Spencer, lived in Norfolk where she became a legendary figure on account of her impish conversation and irrepressible energy (editing the parish magazine at Barton Turf and learning Spanish in her late eighties). Sadly, she died a month before her great-niece's engagement at the age of 91.

It is indeed small wonder that in the light of all these connections, Lady Diana Spencer (as she became styled in 1975 when her father succeeded to the earldom) should have been regarded as the Queen Mother's 'candidate'. Alternative theories along the lines that the Prince of Wales's 'honorary grandfather', Lord Mountbatten, had conspired with Lady Diana's step-grandmother, Barbara Cartland, to promote the Spencer girl's cause do not bear close examination. In

the event, it was singularly appropriate that the two grandmothers and old friends, the Queen Mother and Ruth Lady Fermoy, dined with the happy couple at Clarence House on the night of the engagement.

The present Lord Spencer served King George VI as a temporary equerry in the last two years of the King's life and then carried on in that capacity for the present Queen for another couple of years. He accompanied the Queen and the Duke of Edinburgh as acting Master of the Household on the Commonwealth tour of 1953–54 before returning home to marry Frances Roche. It had been thought in Norfolk that he was likely to marry Lady Anne Coke, daughter of the Earl of Leicester; but it was Lord Fermoy's daughter who walked up the aisle of Westminster Abbey. This location for the ill-fated marriage doubtless affected the Abbey's chances of being used for their youngest daughter's wedding.

A tragedy that may have contributed to the break-up of the marriage was the death of their elder son, John, on the same day that he was born in 1960. In 1967 Lady Althorp (she never became Lady Spencer), left her husband with the four children and they were divorced in 1969. She married Peter Shand Kydd, of the wallpaper family, in the same year. (The divorce has been described as 'difficult'; one might well ask: which one isn't?)

Although Lord Althorp was anxious

to find a mother for his children, he did not remarry until 1976 by which time he had succeeded to the earldom and to the Althorp estate in Northamptonshire. His second wife was the flamboyant former Countess of Dartmouth, a noted figure in the 'heritage' world of preservation and conservation. She helped her new husband sort out the problems of death duties, knocked the house into shape inside and generally made an impact on life at Althorp that was not, perhaps, regarded with universal favour. Whatever Raine's faults, though, her stepchildren are the first to acknowledge the sterling way in which she nursed their father through a severe illness in 1978 that seemed ominous to a degree.

'Johnny' Spencer had a somewhat uneasy relationship with his father 'Jack', who largely devoted himself to caring for the treasures of Althorp. A great connoisseur of the arts, the seventh Earl enjoyed embroidery, sometimes repairing the tapestry chairs himself.

Originally a red-brick moated courtyard house, Althorp's forecourt wings were added in 1575 and the internal courtyard had been covered to become the Grand Staircase by the middle of the seventeenth century. Then the house was Italianized and John Evelyn described the rooms and furnishings as "such as may become a great prince". It continued to be filled with splendid objects, but after the last war the Earl found the place in a bad condition. As James Lees-Milne relates in his diaries "that difficult nobleman" thought of giving Althorp to the National Trust; but instead he set about restoring matters, removing eighteen tons of bedroom walls to reveal seventeenth-century plasterwork and bringing in doors, chimneypieces and so forth from Spencer House in London.

Althorp has often received royal visits, including those of James I's Queen, Anne of Denmark, with her brilliant son, Henry, Prince of Wales (Charles I's elder

brother) *en route* from Holyroodhouse in 1603; William III; the hard-riding Empress Elisabeth of Austria and the late Queen Mary. When she was Duchess of York, the Queen Mother would frequently visit the Spencers when up in Northamptonshire for the hunting season and she returned to Althorp in 1976 to open a special cancer unit nearby which was named after her friend, Cynthia Spencer (the Princess's grandmother).

Today Althorp is, of course, a flourishing showplace under the eagle eye of the present Lady Spencer. The sight of Lord and Lady Spencer serving visitors from far and wide in their shop has helped Althorp become an increasingly popular attraction. The Princess's mother, Mrs Shand Kydd, also has a shop selling farm produce in Scotland.

The Princess's brother, Lord Althorp (as he is styled by courtesy) continued the family's association with the court by doing a stint as a page of honour to the Queen in Silver Jubilee year and subsequently. Lady Sarah, who was one of the Prince of Wales's girl friends and played 'cupid' between him and her sister, is married to a Lincolnshire farmer and former Coldstream Guards officer, Neil McCorquodale, who is, incidentally, a cousin of her stepmother Raine (*née* McCorquodale). Somewhat less

statuesque than her two sisters, Lady Sarah formerly suffered from *anorexia nervosa*. She used to work for Savills, the estate agents and surveyors (it is said that Lady Diana herself did a brief temporary stint there too). By another of those network of coincidences that crop up all the time in these circles, it was in Savills that Lady Jane's father-in-law, Sir William Fellowes, was a partner. Sir William was agent to the Sandringham estate for many years and is a friend of the families of both the Prince and Princess of Wales. In 1977 his son, Robert, became assistant private secretary to the Queen and the following year he married Lady Jane Spencer, who had previously worked as a fashion assistant on *Vogue*.

The wedding was duly chronicled by the indestructible 'Jennifer' in *Harpers &*
Queen and sharp royalty watchers could note that among the bridesmaids in a group picture at the reception in St James's Palace which included the Queen Mother, the Gloucesters and the Duchess of Kent stood Lady Diana. The photograph was taken by Sir Geoffrey Shakerley, whose brother-in-law, the ubiquitous Earl of Lichfield, was to do the honours at a somewhat larger affair three years later. And so the court circled around the youngest Spencer girl.

The Princess's Spencer ancestors alone have numbered three Lord Chamberlains, as well as a Groom of the Stole; George III and Queen Charlotte were godparents to one of the daughters of the second Earl; Queen Victoria was godmother to another Spencer girl. It would not be easy to cite any other family so replete with royal connections. From

The wedding groups of the Princess's sisters, Lady Jane Fellowes (left) and Lady Sarah McCorquodale (above)

Below: Lady Sarah Spencer at Smith's Lawn polo ground with the Prince of Wales and at Cowes with Prince Edward
Opposite: Frances Shand Kydd rides with Prince Philip after the royal wedding; Lady Diana with Prince Andrew on the way to the Birthday Parade in 1981

early childhood it could be said that the Princess was at least on the fringes of the world in which she now occupies centre stage. The Spencer children played with the royal children and went to each other's birthday parties at Sandringham. Princes Andrew and Edward were among Diana's earliest friends and playmates. "I always ganged up with Prince Andrew," she recalled. The Queen was apparently called "Aunt Lilibet".

Such evidence of propinquity and intimacy confirms that the Princess was tailor-made for the job – indeed the 'girl-next-door' as she has been called by some. It is almost as if she had a royal destiny.

DIEU·DEFEND·LE·DROIT

Blood Royal and Rare

The Princess of Wales is the first English bride of the heir to the throne since 1659 when Lady Anne Hyde, daughter of the Earl of Clarendon, married the future James II. However, Lady Anne (the mother of Queens Anne and Mary II) never became Queen, dying in 1671, and one has to go back to the wives of Henry VIII to find the last English Queen consort. The Hanoverians married German princesses; Queen Alexandra was Danish; Queen Mary was another German and the Queen Mother, though born in London (and, incidentally, having a lesser proportion of blood from north of the border than the Princess of Wales), is regarded as Scottish.

The Princess's ancestry is naturally of great interest, bearing in mind that her lines are now part of the royal genealogy. She is descended from four Kings from whom the Prince of Wales is not, so she brings back their blood into the Royal Family. These Kings are Henry IV (from whom she is descended through Antigone, the illegitimate daughter of 'Good Duke Humphrey' of Gloucester, whose library is now housed in the Bodleian at Oxford); Charles I, Charles II and James II. The Princess has three certain descents from Charles II (plus two doubtful ones from the dashing Duke of Monmouth's sister Mary Sarsfield), and one from James II through his liaison with Arabella Churchill, as well as a descent from Elizabeth, the 'Winter Queen' of Bohemia, the daughter of James I. The

Princess's other royal ancestors include Henry IV of France and Henry VII of England, from whom she is descended many times over.

She has several ancestors in common with the Prince of Wales, but their closest relationship is that of seventh cousin once removed, through their descent from the third Duke of Devonshire. Her paternal ancestry is widely representative of the eighteenth-century Whig oligarchy. Setting aside the tenuous claims of descent from the medieval Despensers, the Spencers are a comparatively 'new' family as aristocratic families go, in that their first recorded ancestor is Sir John Spencer, a man of substance at the beginning of the Tudor period. The family had become rich through sheep and Sir John bought the Wormleighton estate in Warwickshire and the Althorp estate in Northamptonshire early in the sixteenth century. "My Lord, when these things were doing your ancestors were keeping sheep," said the 'Collecting Earl' of Arundel to the first Lord Spencer during a Parliamentary debate in 1621; to which Lord Spencer riposted: "When my ancestors were keeping sheep, Your Lordship's ancestors were plotting treason."

The first Lord Spencer was reputed to have more ready money than anyone else in the kingdom thanks to his 19,000 sheep and to his shrewd dealings in cattle, rye and barley. The second Lord Spencer's wife was the daughter of Shakespeare's patron the Earl of Southampton and their eldest son, Henry, married the poet Waller's 'Sacharissa'. The Cavalier Henry lent Charles I £10,000 at the beginning of the Civil War and was created Earl of Sunderland, only to be killed four months later at the Battle of Newbury. His son, the brilliant and much feared second Earl of Sunderland, was the wily lieutenant of Charles II, James II and William III. He had a remarkably varied career and was generally regarded as the craftiest, most rapacious and most unscrupulous of all the politicians of the second half of the seventeenth century.

The third Earl of Sunderland married the daughter of the great Duke of Marlborough and their children included an earlier Lady Diana Spencer, who was a strong candidate to become the bride of George II's unsatisfactory son 'Poor Fred', the Prince of Wales. The match was frustrated by the first 'Prime Minister' Sir Robert Walpole (himself an ancestor, incidentally, of the later Lady Diana). Lady Diana's brother Charles succeeded to the Dukedom of Marlborough and the Blenheim estates, whereas their brother John inherited the Spencer family property and was ancestor of the Earls Spencer. John also benefited from the generosity of his formidable grandmother, Sarah Duchess of Marlborough, who left him the Marlborough Plate.

The first Earl Spencer, who built

Spencer House overlooking Green Park in London, was a friend of the circle that included Sir Joshua Reynolds who painted his wife and their daughter Georgiana, the beautiful and scandalous Duchess of Devonshire ('the face without a frown'). The second Earl, First Lord of the Admiralty at the time of Trafalgar, had Henry Holland, the fashionable Whig architect, remodel Althorp. The third Earl was also a successful politician, becoming Chancellor of the Exchequer and promoting the Reform Bill, but his main love was farming. The next Earl was an Admiral and took an old salt's view of discipline; when his daughter was disobedient, he did not hesitate to lock her up in a cupboard under the stairs. His son was known as 'Red Earl' on account of his long red beard and the Seymour girl whom the Red Earl married came to be known as 'Spencer's Fairy Queen'. The Red Earl did a couple of stints as Lord Lieutenant of Ireland, but was happiest in the hunting field.

The Princess's paternal lines of ancestry yield some impressive names such as the Field-Marshals Anglesey, who lost a leg at Waterloo, and Lucan of the Heavy Brigade; the Restoration rake Rochester; Admiral Howe; the second Earl Grey; and Grenville of the *Revenge*. She has a fair measure of Welsh blood through her descent from Lady Dorothy Vaughan and can actually claim direct descent from the great Owen Glendower himself. As Duchess of Cornwall, it is appropriate that she is also a direct descendant of that Cornish hero Bishop Trelawny – one of the 'Seven Bishops' imprisoned in the Tower of London for refusing to subscribe to the Declaration of Indulgence in 1688 and triumphantly acquitted of seditious libel. It is interesting, too, that the Princess is a collateral descendant of all Henry VIII's English Queens.

On her mother's side, the Princess's ancestry presents a strikingly different picture being almost entirely Irish and

Opposite: The Prince and Princess with the Duke and Duchess of Marlborough at the Princess's ancestral home, Blenheim Palace
Below: 'The face without a frown': Georgiana, Duchess of Devonshire, daughter of the first Earl Spencer

Scottish, with an influx of American New England pioneer stock. The Roche family were originally Roman Catholic, but the first Lord Fermoy, whose mother is said to have been a relation of Edward Burke, conformed to the established church. The Princess's Irish ancestors include the O'Donovans; the Hennessys; the eccentric Coghlans of Ardo, whose collateral lines embraced Marshal Macmahon, President of France in the early years of the Third Republic; and Timothy Deasy, the first Catholic magistrate to be appointed (in 1793). The Fermoys' principal seat was the windswept Trabolgan overlooking the sea near Whitegate, County Cork. In a south-easterly gale it is a considerable struggle to open the hall door; thus, in the winter, the family would repair to the fine Palladian house inland of Kilshannig.

The first Lord Fermoy's wife was a Boothby and the Princess derives various Huguenot descents from this line. The second Lord Fermoy sold up in Ireland about a hundred years ago and his brother, who became the third Baron, married the daughter of a New York banker, Frank Work. The Works had originated in Scotland and the most notable American lines in the Princess's ancestry come through Frank Work's mother-in-law Ellen Strong, whose father invented and patented the axle tourniquet for the control of bleeding during surgical operations. Dr Joseph Strong's ancestry can be traced in all

lines to New England pioneers (most of whom came from England in the seventeenth century). Thanks to this, the Princess can claim relationships with eight Presidents of the United States, as well as to such diverse figures as Louisa M. Alcott, Humphrey Bogart, Mrs Rudolph Valentino, John Pierpont Morgan, General George Patton, Ralph Waldo Emerson, the Gish sisters, Orson Welles and others too humorous to mention.

A royal wedding is one of those occasions when genealogists come out from the woodwork of family trees and much fun has been had working out

bizarre cousinships for the Princess. Among her other unexpected kinsfolk and connections, for example, are Mrs Fitzherbert, Oliver Cromwell, Lawrence of Arabia, Byron, Darwin, Jane Austen, Lewis Carroll, Pepys, Swift, Wordsworth, David Niven, Caruso, Richard Ingrams, Auberon Waugh, Giscard d'Estaing, the Red Baron, Bluebeard and the Marquis de Sade. It can even be worked out that the Princess is a fifteenth cousin once removed of the Duchess of Windsor, but when it comes down to it, relationships of this distance can be applied to almost anybody.

Young England

"A superb physical specimen" is how Diana's father describes her as a baby. She weighed in at 7 lb 12 oz at Park House, Sandringham, on 1 July 1961. Here she enjoyed a pleasantly rural childhood complete with a nanny and plenty of outdoor life, including the care of a succession of little furry creatures from hamsters to guinea pigs. Her father has recollected her development into a practical little girl with an eye for what needed doing about the place. Park House is situated beyond Sandringham Church and affords plenty of opportunities for exploring among the rhododendrons and off the beaten tracks of the estate avenues.

After the arrival of her baby brother Charles in 1964, Diana joined her sisters in the schoolroom at Park House which was under the supervision of Gertrude Allen, or 'Ally'. Other children from the estate also came here for their educational grounding; past pupils include the Princess's brother-in-law, Robert Fellowes. Before her death Ally said that Diana was a serious little girl who tried hard, being particularly fond of history and stories about kings and queens – "not battles" – as well as fairy-tales with happy endings.

There was to be an unhappy ending, though, to the story of her parents' marriage and from 1967 onwards Diana had to face life without the constant presence of her mother. However, she was to spend pleasant holidays with her mother and new step-father before long, as life settled into a new pattern. First, Diana went to a day-school, Silfield, in Kings Lynn and then as a boarder to Riddlesworth Hall, a preparatory school near Diss.

Her father, an avid photographer, duly recorded the poignant moment as his youngest daughter sat elegantly on the trunk marked 'D F Spencer'. Soon her shoulder-length hair would be cut to regulation length as she tried to live up to the school motto by 'facing forward'. Riddlesworth, which is owned by the Noel family, was rebuilt along classical lines after a fire at the turn of this century. The headmistress in Diana's day was the long-serving Elisabeth Ridsdale ('Riddy') who remembers the Princess as being "good at games, especially swimming". In Riddy's words, Diana was "always a decent, kind and happy little girl. Everyone seemed to like her . . . She took part in everything . . . What stands out in my mind is how awfully sweet she was with the little ones." Lord Spencer felt these qualities outweighed any shortcomings in her school work. However, she was to pass her common entrance examination to a public school of above average academic standards without any difficulty.

Diana's prep school friends included Alexandra Loyd, a Sandringham neighbour as her father is the Queen's land agent, and Lord Suffield's daughter, Caroline Harbord-Hamond, who went on to West Heath near Sevenoaks with Diana. Both these girls now have jobs in the political world, Alexandra Loyd working for Tory whizz-kid John Patten. Other West Heath friends included Mary-Ann Stewart-Richardson, also from Norfolk, and Carolyn Pride, who shared Diana's passion for music.

This feeling for music comes from both sides of the family as her grandmother Ruth Lady Fermoy was a concert pianist and her Spencer great-aunt Lady Delia Peel played the 'cello. The Princess herself has perfect pitch and names Tchaikovsky and Greig as among her favourite composers. "I am obsessed with ballet", she has said. "I always wanted to be a ballet dancer and started taking lessons when I was three and a half. But I just grew too tall. I didn't take exams, I just enjoyed dancing." Carolyn Pride, whose father lived near the school at Tenterden, went on to the Royal College of Music and, of course, to share the flat with Lady Diana.

At West Heath Carolyn was a prefect and played lacrosse for the school, while Diana captained the hockey team and won various swimming and diving cups. Her headmistress, Ruth Rudge, an Australian, said of Diana: "She's a girl who notices what needs to be done, then does it willingly and cheerfully." In her last year, Lady Diana (as she was then styled) received an award for service: "We don't give this every year," commented Miss Rudge. "It's presented

only to outstanding pupils ... I think Diana was surprised she'd won it.''

A colour photograph of the Prince of Wales in his Investiture regalia decorated the dormitory in which his future wife slept. Inevitably some of her contemporaries are prepared to come forward with bitchy reminiscences about her allegedly aloof manner, her nickname of 'Duchess' and her lack of scholastic prowess; but she is warmly remembered by those who knew her as cheerful and eternally willing to help.

She visited an old lady near the school regularly to lend a hand with the shopping and the domestic chores, as well as helping out at a centre for handicapped children.

In the school holidays she would divide her time between her mother's home on the Isle of Seil and, from 1975 onwards, Althorp. It was at Althorp one weekend in November 1977 that she encountered the Prince of Wales in a ploughed field. The Prince was shooting with the Spencers and remembered

thinking "what a very jolly and amusing and attractive sixteen-year-old she was."

The following January, Lady Diana went to be 'finished' in Switzerland at the Institut Alpin Videmanette at Château d'Oex near Gstaad but, though she learned to ski and brushed up on her French, she only stayed one term. In London she lived for a spell in her mother's flat in Cadogan Place, sharing with Tory MP Marcus Kimball's daughter, Sophie, but decided against 'coming out' as a debutante in the tawdry travesty that passes itself off as the London 'season'.

Lady Diana already knew what she wanted in life. She wanted to work with children and then she intended to marry and have children of her own. This special rapport she has with children is a vital facet of her character. Even at school, as we have seen, she was noted for looking after the little ones. A touching feature of the royal wedding was how strongly the nation's children identified with their beloved Lady Diana.

She cut her teeth as a part-time nanny, forming a particular attachment to a two-year-old American boy living in London. Then, after doing a cookery course with Elizabeth Russell in Wimbledon and various bits and pieces, she settled down to a regular job in a nursery school, the Young England Kindergarten in Pimlico. Initially Lady Diana (or 'Miss Diana' as she was known to the 50 or so children under five there) came in on the odd afternoon, then mornings, and finally on a three-day-a-week basis. The school is run by Kay Seth-Smith and Victoria Wilson is the headmistress; pupils included Diana Rigg's daughter, Rachel. "She enjoys children enormously", said Kay Seth-Smith of Lady Diana.

Until the attentions of the media made it impossible for her, Lady Diana would bicycle to and from the flat in Coleherne Court that her parents had bought for her. She moved into the block about the time of her eighteenth birthday in July 1979 together with Carolyn Pride; they were soon joined by Ann Bolton, a secretary with Savills, and Virginia Pitman, the youngest of four daughters of a former Major in the 11th Hussars (or 'Cherry Pickers') from Yorkshire. Ann Bolton recalled that they "worked as a team", though they had their own friends and their own lives. Nonetheless, as Carolyn Pride observed of Lady Diana: "We'd spend evening after evening after evening content in each other's company, as are we all." Virginia Pitman has memories of coming back to the flat and finding Lady Diana "dancing around the flat, just on her own, bopping around".

This jolly closed world of the girls' flat acted as a sort of chrysalis in which Lady Diana developed before blossoming out into the limelight. Life at Coleherne Court had many of the characteristics of the 'Sloane Ranger' syndrome. According to the *Tatler*, dinner party conversation concentrated on "Benetton sale bargains, which friend is working in Parrots and who's just had their bicycle stolen", as well as shooting and riding. (Lady Diana's own equestrian experiences were marred by her breaking an arm in a fall as a little girl.) Friends tended to be in estate agencies, the wine trade or the auction houses. For the occasional foray out, favoured restaurants included the *Poule au Pot* in Ebury Street and *Topolino d'Ischia* in Draycott Avenue. The 'set', such as it was, were too nice and ordinary to appear in the gossip columns.

To the names already mentioned can be added the tall figure of Harry Herbert, the stockbroker son of the Queen's racing manager Lord Porchester (himself the son of that rakish old self-publicist Lord Carnarvon), and his sister Carolyn; Humphrey Butler of Christie's; Theresa Mowbray, a goddaughter of Mrs Shand Kydd and a year senior to Lady Diana at West Heath; and Simon Berry of the wine brotherhood. Berry and Herbert were involved in the amateur revival of that quintessentially 1950s play *The Reluctant Debutante* by William Douglas-Home (a cousin of the Princess, it need hardly be said).

The Princess's chums have remained

admirably discreet about her private life, unlike so many of the people around the Prince of Wales's former girl-friends. Virginia Pitman has said that "quite a few men were quite keen", but the press has only picked up a couple of other male leads. *Private Eye* pointed out that James Boughey of the Coldstream Guards, who played cricket for Eton, had been Lady Diana's constant companion before 'Brian' (as the Prince is known in the *Eye*) came on the scene; whereas the *Daily Mirror* picked on George Plumptre, a younger son of Lord FitzWalter, who wrote a handsome work on *Royal Gardens* and was among the guests at the royal wedding.

Sylvie Krin of *Private Eye* has provided by far the most readable and amusing – and not necessarily all that wide of the mark in places – account of the royal romance in *Born to be Queen*, but we have to try to stick to some of the facts. Inevitably, again, there have been conveniently anonymous 'friends' ready to testify that Lady Diana had been secretly in love with the Prince for some years before he finally noticed her: "She was so obviously mad about him. He started by being rather touched by it. Then when he saw how well she handled the publicity he started to take her seriously." The 'friend' continued to the effect that the Prince would be "as much in love as she is" by the time the wedding day dawned.

Anyway, in August 1979, Lady Diana went north to join the royal house-party at Balmoral. She was there when the terrible news came through about the assassination of Lord Mountbatten in Ireland. The following February, Lady Diana travelled to Sandringham with Mountbatten's granddaughter Amanda

Opposite: Royal retreat: Balmoral Castle
Below left: Diana watching polo at Cowdray
Right: Disliking the prying cameras at Windsor

(apparently known as the 'long-stop' in the Princess of Wales competition) for another royal house-party. On both occasions Lady Diana was ostensibly present as a companion for her old friend Prince Andrew.

However, in the summer of 1980 it began to look as if the Prince of Wales had other ideas. He asked Lady Diana to watch him play polo at Cowdray in July; Cowes week found her on board the *Britannia* and in the first week of September she was up at Balmoral again. As the Prince said later: "We began to realize there was something in it." A photographer caught Lady Diana watching the Prince fishing for salmon in the Dee and suddenly, irrevocably, her life was changed. She was no longer a private person.

Public Property

From September 1980 to February 1981 Lady Diana had to run the royal hacks' gauntlet. With hindsight this appalling ordeal for a nineteen-year-old girl can be said to have been a test, though presumably it was not meant to be. As her proud father, Lord Spencer, said: "She came through with flying colours."

Pursued night and day, up hill and down dale – even through a school lavatory window in one instance – the press's quarry was hunted down. The 'H' block of Coleherne Court was under constant siege and Lady Diana's publicly listed telephone number was naturally taken full advantage of. "All this fuss is disrupting my work with the children," pointed out Lady Diana to pressmen at the Young England Kindergarten. In the hope of keeping the photographers quiet, she posed with two of the children in the gardens in front of the school; the result was the notorious 'see through' portfolio.

Everyone became aware of this strikingly tall and lovely girl in the Prince's life. Lady Diana had certainly blossomed beautifully from the gawky schoolgirl she had been a few years before. In spite of all the pressures she got on with life in her quietly determined manner. She had her own special way with journalists: "I love working with children, and I have learned to be very patient with them. I simply treat the press as though they were children."

Somehow she managed to keep

seeing the Prince in secret. In October she was in Scotland again with him and the Queen Mother. The Prince gave her a copy of his best-selling story for children (originally written for Prince Edward), *The Old Man of Lochnagar.* Other sightings of Lady Diana with the Prince occurred at Ludlow Races, at the Wiltshire home of the Prince's friends the Parker Bowleses and at the Ritz for Princess Margaret's 50th birthday party. Speculation mounted to fever pitch as the Prince's 32nd birthday loomed nearer – how he had been haunted by his remark that around 30 was the age to marry.

Then the *Sunday Mirror* came out with the extraordinary allegation that Lady Diana had spent the night after the Ritz party on the royal train with the Prince who was on an official visit to the West Country. This caused a major rumpus and the Queen's press secretary demanded an apology which was not forthcoming. Lady Diana told the attendant hacks at the kindergarten that the story was completely false: "I stayed in that evening with my flatmates. That is the absolute truth. I had some supper and watched television before going to bed early." The strain, inevitably, was beginning to tell. She told a woman who lived in Coleherne Court that "the whole thing has got out of control . . . I am not so much bored as miserable. Everywhere I go there is someone there . . . If I go to a restaurant or just out shopping in the supermarket they are trying to take photographs." The woman, of course, turned out to be a journalist herself.

Stephen Pile of the *Sunday Times* had the happy notion of sending a reporter to badger the *Sunday Mirror*'s editor to see how he liked it, which he did not. Some repentant hacks slipped a note of apology into Lady Diana's red Mini-Metro – by now the most familiar motor-car in the country – after she had been reduced to tears in Berkeley Square. The Prince of Wales went off to India and Nepal, but still the persecution by the 'leg-men' (as they are known in Fleet Street) continued. The whole thing had indeed got out of control and Lady Diana's mother, Mrs Shand Kydd, was moved to write to *The Times* asking if it was "necessary or fair to harass my daughter daily from dawn until well after dusk." Was it "fair to ask any human being, regardless of circumstances, to be treated in this way?"

Without taking the line of 'we are all guilty', the trouble was we all wanted to know too much. This is the price the Royal Family has to pay for being so popular. What was so distasteful about the hounding of Lady Diana was that she was not even a member of the Royal Family and had to face the constant glare of publicity alone. The truth of the intolerable situation was probably that the media had jumped in with both feet just as the relationship was in its infancy. This led to the Prince of Wales coming

under fire for leaving Lady Diana so exposed, for dithering about a proposal and so on. Tempers began to fray as the press invaded Sandringham after Christmas in the hope of seeing the arrival of Lady Diana. The Queen herself was driven to raise her voice to photographers as they hovered near a Shetland pony ridden by young Peter Phillips: "I do wish you would go away." The Prince of Wales wished "a particularly nasty" New Year to the journalists' editors.

Later in January, Lady Diana lunched with the Prince at his house in Gloucestershire, Highgrove, and met him at his trainer's stables early one morning when he rode out on his ill-fated horse, Allibar. They managed to give the pressmen the slip back at Sandringham and then the Prince went off on his own, ski-ing with the Palmer-Tomkinsons in Switzerland. Lady Diana was soon to head for an Australian holiday at the Shand Kydds' sheep farm; but, at long last, the Prince's proposal was made after dinner in his

rooms in Buckingham Palace on 5 February. He said later: "I asked Diana before she went to Australia ... because I thought it would be a good idea that, apart from anything else, if she went to Australia she could then think about it. And if she didn't like the idea, she could say she didn't or she did." In fact she accepted him before she went to Australia.

Their engagement remained a secret, though Lady Diana told her flatmates before flying out *incognito* with her mother and stepfather to Sydney. But the press even tracked them down in the outback and they had to retreat to a beach house, where the holiday atmosphere cannot have been helped by the dread of ending up in the goldfish bowl yet again. However, Mrs Shand Kydd has said it was "like a real family holiday", with swimming and surfing. She was determined to have "what my daughter and I knew to be our last holiday together". Naturally they talked about Lady Diana's future life which

*Below: Lady Diana leaving the Lambourn home of
Nick Gaselee, the Prince's racehorse trainer
Opposite: Outside Coleherne Court*

now lay like a long red carpet before her.

After slipping back quietly to England, Lady Diana was watching the morning's exercise at Lambourn when the Prince's beloved Allibar collapsed and died. It was a shared emotional experience for the couple, as Judy Gaselee, the trainer's wife told the press: "She stood with tears running down her cheeks as Charles knelt by the horse. They were both obviously very upset." Allibar had been due to run at Chepstow that afternoon and was the Prince's only horse in his spirited attempt to come to terms with the splendid sport of steeplechasing. Nick Gaselee, his trainer, had previously been assistant to the Queen Mother's stalwart of the jumping game, Fulke Walwyn, and Lady Diana's newly forged friendship with the family was sealed by their daughter, Sarah Jane, becoming her bridesmaid.

On the following day, Saturday 21 February, the Prince duly telephoned Lady Diana's father to ask for his youngest daughter's hand ("I wonder what he would have said if I had said no," the engaging Earl commented later). On the Sunday the Prince gave his betrothed the engagement ring – described by Lady Diana as "a wonderful sapphire and diamonds" – and on the Tuesday morning came the official announcement by the Queen and the Duke of Edinburgh.

The crowd outside Buckingham Palace was found to contain Lord and Lady Spencer. He forecast that it would be easier for Lady Diana from then on: "She will be under some protection, whereas before she had to face the music on her own." With the Prince at her side, the object of world-wide fascination faced the press in a sapphire silk suit (bought off the peg at Harrods) that was to become the best-known piece of clothing in living memory. Lady Diana said she felt the pressure "and every-

thing" had been worthwhile – "every bit of it". She hoped that she had "coped all right" and her interviewers spoke for us all when they said everyone was full of admiration for the way she had done so.

The Prince said he felt "just delighted and happy. I'm amazed that she's been brave enough to take me on." However, he struck rather the wrong note with his reply to the (admittedly fatuous) question about whether they were 'in love' – "whatever 'in love' means".

What the engagement meant for Lady Diana was that a velvet curtain came down on her old life: she gave up her job at the kindergarten, she left Coleherne Court and began her induction course as a royal personage. The curriculum was concerned with the intricacies of royal protocol and some of the problems could not have been familiar to her tutors as there had not been a Princess of Wales for 71 years.

Lady Diana's mother, Mrs Shand Kydd, commented that "It's an unknown world for her, but I'm sure she can cope and learn very quickly." Although it was assumed that Lady Diana had moved into Clarence House for the duration – following the grandmothers' celebration dinner – she only stayed there for a few days before settling into a secret address in Pimlico from where she commuted to a suite at Buckingham Palace. Here she grappled with the niceties of state procedure, venturing out to assemble her trousseau with her mother. Cut off from the cosy existence of Coleherne Court, she wrote to a friend: "life in Buckingham Palace isn't bad. But too many formal dinners (yuk!)."

*Below: Lady Diana with Princess Grace of Monaco
and the Prince of Wales at Goldsmiths' Hall
Opposite: Sporting supporter at Cowdray (left) and
Sandown (right)*

After a weekend with the Cholmondeleys in Cheshire, the Prince and Lady Diana went out together to Covent Garden to see Grace Bumbry in *L'Africaine*, the opera by Meyerbeer. Earlier that day, 3 March, it had been announced – much to the chagrin of Stanley Gibbons who had already rushed out a special 'royal wedding' catalogue featuring Westminster Abbey on the front – that the ceremony was to take place in St Paul's Cathedral. This was regarded as something of a surprise, but, on examination, the reasons were manifold. Both the Prince and Lady Diana loved the Cathedral (designed, incidentally, by her fourth cousin nine times removed, Sir Christopher Wren), with its marvellous musical acoustics; it accommodates more guests and has a better position than the Abbey. Moreover, the Abbey had unfortunate associations through Lady Diana's divorced parents marrying there as well as Lord Mountbatten's funeral, whereas St Paul's evoked the joy of the Silver Wedding, Silver Jubilee

and the Queen Mother's 80th birthday celebrations.

At the beginning of the next week came what the *Tatler* described as 'the greatest moment of sexual theatre since Cinderella leapt out of her clapped-out scullery clogs into her glass slippers' when Lady Diana attended a charity gala in aid of the Royal Opera House at Goldsmiths' Hall in the City of London wearing – or almost wearing – a strapless black silk taffeta ballgown. In the words of the perennially anonymous 'fellow guest', the message from Lady Diana was clear: 'Don't think I'm just suitable. I'm gorgeous as well.' It was certainly a magnificent gesture, cocking a snook at the prurient and squashing the 'Shy Di'

image. Amidst a dribble of jokes about 'See Nipples and Di', Independent Television News regaled us with a slow motion action replay to determine whether or not a certain something or other on her bosom was a shadow or whatever.

Writing in the *International Herald Tribune*, Lady Windlesham (otherwise Prudence Glynn, former fashion editor of *The Times*) thought that Lady Diana had committed "a social gaffe" and that the dress made her look as if she was sitting in a hip bath. In an amazing outburst, Lady Windlesham called Lady Diana "a fashion disaster in her own right". The impact that the Princess of Wales has had on the whole fashion

industry from her haircut down to her knickerbockers would rather fly in the face of Lady Windlesham's strictures.

The controversial black dress was the work of David and Elizabeth Emanuel, a husband and wife team operating in Brook Street. The Emanuels had built up a reputation – thanks to Princess Michael of Kent and various showbiz figures – for elaborately romantic gowns. Now they were to be given the most sought-after commission of all, the royal wedding dress. Lady Diana's team of stylists for the great day were to be equally young and unstuffy: hair by Kevin Shanley of Headlines in South Kensington; make-up by Barbara Daly, the television beautician; and shoes by Clive Shilton of Covent Garden.

Lady Diana did not seem too happy in the obligatory headgear of royalty to begin with and she appeared, understandably, somewhat ill at ease on her behatted outing to see the Prince ride in a race at Sandown. Racegoers warmed to her coltish charm, though, and sympathized with her concern over the luckless Prince's fall on – or rather off – his new horse, Good Prospect. Judy Gaselee took charge of Lady Diana in the unsaddling enclosure afterwards and steered her adroitly away from the crush. Those who waited in the rain outside the royal box at the end of racing were rewarded with a vignette of sorts. A cheerful punter greeted the lady as "Di" only to be admonished blushingly, but firmly, that the name was "Diana"; a faintly embarrassing situation was retrieved by a jocular remark from the Prince.

Lady Diana reacted more sympathetically when approached by young Nicholas Hardy at Dean Close School with the question: "May I kiss the hand of my future Queen?" "Yes, you may," she replied, extending her hand. "You will never live this down," she added as his fellow pupils sniggered. That after-noon, 27 March, the Queen gave her formal consent to the marriage at a meeting of the Privy Council at Buckingham Palace. Afterwards Her Majesty posed for her first official photographs with the Prince and Lady Diana in the Music Room and it was noticeable how the latter towered not only over the diminutive sovereign but also apparently over her future husband – a disparity that had been adjusted in the pose for the ubiquitous engagement picture by Lady Diana standing on a lower step outside the Palace.

Two days later the Prince was off on his travels again; this time on a five-week tour of Australia, Venezuela and America. It was thought that while in Australia he would be sounding out the possibilities of becoming Governor-General. In the event, while Malcolm Fraser, the Prime Minister, and his coalition government seemed to favour the idea, the Australian Labour Party remained unconvinced that the job could be kept out of the political fray. The matter looked as if it might get an unwelcome public airing when Simon Regan, a freelance journalist and erstwhile biographer of the Prince, started touting some tapes of alleged telephone conversations recorded between the Prince in Australia and Lady Diana. Farrers, the royal solicitors, moved in swiftly with a writ and obtained an injunction preventing the publication of the tapes in Britain. But by the time the *Irish Independent* printed the material for the benefit of readers in the British Isles, it was manifestly clear that the whole thing was a hoax; the dialogue was absurdly unconvincing and stuffed with silly solecisms.

Back in England the Prince took his betrothed to Broadlands – where they were to spend the first night of their married life – to open an exhibition on the life of Lord Mountbatten and plant a pair of Atlantic cedars. Lady Diana appeared to be in her element, kneeling

*Below: The official photograph following the Queen's
formal consent*

*Below left: The Prince says goodbye at Heathrow
before flying to the Antipodes*
*Below right: Posies for the prospective Princess on
her visit to her future hometown, Tetbury*
*Opposite: At Ascot with the perennially popular
Princess Alexandra*

unselfconsciously to chat with children, accepting flowers and generally behaving in a way that can indeed only be described as enchanting. A walk-about to meet her prospective neighbours in Tetbury was another personal triumph for Lady Diana, as she picked up a baby, took posies, shook hands and posed for photographs in a manner that any politician would envy. Quite simply, the more the nation saw of its future Queen, the more they fell in love with her. "I

couldn't have married anyone the British people wouldn't have liked," said the Prince. It was now surely true that he couldn't have married anyone the British people would have liked more.

As the busy royal summer programme got into full swing Lady Diana was, needless to say, the main attraction whether practising her 'royal wave' at Ascot or bringing a humorous touch to a garden party; at the Birthday Parade (Trooping the Colour), State Banquets, Royal Academy soirée or at Wimbledon. The day before her twentieth birthday, she was at a garden party for hundreds of tenants of the Duchy of Cornwall at Highgrove. Earlier in June she had seen one of her future bridesmaids, Clementine Hambro (Sir Winston Churchill's little great-granddaughter), get in some practice at the wedding of the Prince's fat

friend, Nicholas Soames, to Catherine Weatherall. Again with hindsight, Lady Diana was probably asked to do too much in the busy run-up to the wedding. Being 'engaged' even in normal circumstances is an anxious period, bad for the nerves and neither one thing nor the other; but to be stared at everywhere you go by hundreds or thousands of strange people and to be expected to react pleasantly the whole time was bound to cause excessive strain.

Even the experienced Prince of Wales admitted to a military gathering at Tidworth the week before the wedding that he had "got to the stage where I feel I am disappearing up through my own fundamental". Observers noticed that Lady Diana was darting frequent furtive sideways glances – a mannerism that one journalist has pointed out makes her

*Below: The royal couple at Smith's Lawn, Windsor
Opposite: A strikingly thinner Lady Diana leaves St
Paul's with her betrothed after the wedding rehearsal*

appear to have no eyeballs when seen from the side. It was on the next day at a polo match that Lady Diana had to retreat from a phalanx of photographers, temporarily overcome with tears.

The thousands of letters that poured into the Palace daily cheered her on and she was particularly touched by the presents "that have come from children who have obviously spent hours of work on paintings, pictures, cards, anything like that, and things they've baked at home; it's wonderful". She had also received a collage from the children when she went to the end of term party at Young England: "I ended up being battered and bruised; I had so many children crawling on top of me. But they presented me with that and a glass representing Young England. It was lovely, really nice." The Prince of Wales reckoned that they had received about 100,000 letters and over 3000 presents. Lady Diana had experienced the ups and downs of being a piece of public property.

On the eve of the wedding she moved back into Clarence House to stay with the Queen Mother, having told television viewers she would be "tucked up in bed" while the fireworks were lighting the sky above Hyde Park. It was a steamily pulsating night; outside her windows and along the Mall the carnival atmosphere generated an electric buzz of excitement.

The Wedding

"We still cannot get over what happened that day," said the Prince of Wales, recalling the wonder of 29 July 1981. "Neither of us can get over the atmosphere; it was electric, I felt, and so did my wife." Outside his window at Buckingham Palace the noise had been "almost indescribable". Since then he had stood at the same window trying to remember it "so I can tell my children what it was like".

"I remember several occasions that were similar, with large crowds: the Coronation and Jubilee, and various major national occasions," said the Prince. "All of them were special in their own way but our wedding was quite extraordinary as far as we were concerned. It made us both, and we have discussed it several times, extraordinarily proud to be British."

The day was not only "quite extraordinary" for the Prince and Princess but for the millions who watched from all over the world; there was indeed something in the air that made one glad to be alive. The Prince said before the wedding that he wanted everybody to leave St Paul's having had "a marvellous musical and emotional experience" and in the event it was not just the guests inside the Cathedral who did so. Many an unlikely figure was moved to tears. The trouble with such magnificent occasions when, as Yehudi Menuhin said, "each of us is transformed into a joyful member of the human brotherhood," is that the transformation only lasts a day. It is impossible to capture the feelings in words at the time and any attempts to do so later inevitably cause embarrassment to our essentially introvert natures.

The pictures, though, live on to remind us of the marvellous images and impressions we formed on that perfect summer's day. Above all, the sight of what her father fittingly called the "fairly-tale Princess". Before leaving his flat, Lord Spencer obliged the media once more with a statement: "The Spencers have through the centuries fought for their King and country. Today Diana is vowing to help her country for the rest of her life. She will be following in the tradition of her ancestors and she will have at her side the man she loves." His own courage and determination, masked by a touching delight in the whole show, to play his role in the proceedings despite his poor health was certainly one of the features of the day.

The bride's father went to Clarence House to escort his daughter to the Cathedral in the Glass Coach (built in 1910 when the sixth Earl Spencer was Lord Chamberlain). Some spectators, eager to get a first glimpse of the bride in her wedding dress, were disappointed to discover that this is, of course, a covered coach. The bride wore a flamboyantly romantic dress of ivory pure silk taffeta; the bodice had a frilled neckline with embroidered lace panels at front and back and the 25-foot train was trimmed and edged with sparkling lace. That ruffle which Lady Diana had already made her hallmark was the focal point of this almost theatrically fairy-tale creation. The bridesmaids wore garlands in their hair, Victorian-style dresses and carried baskets of meadow flowers; while the pages were kitted out in Victorian naval uniform. The chief bridesmaid was Princess Margaret's daughter, Lady Sarah Armstrong-Jones, an experienced hand; the others were Lord

Mountbatten's granddaughter, India Hicks, Sarah Jane Gaselee and the two young ones, Catherine Cameron (aged six) and Clementine Hambro (five). India and Catherine are both goddaughters of the Prince of Wales. The smart pages were the Duke of Kent's younger son, Lord Nicholas Windsor and Edward van Cutsem, grandson of the late Bernard van Cutsem, the trainer, and son of the bridegroom's friend, Hugh, who had been to the fore at the Prince's 'bachelor dinner' at White's the previous week. All present and correct, the bridesmaids and pages left by car for St Paul's from Clarence House at 10.20 and the bride's procession set out a quarter of an hour later. The official escort was provided by the Mounted Police as Lady Diana was not yet a royal personage.

Meanwhile the guests had been assembling in the Cathedral. The space allocated for the bride's side had not, perhaps, been over-generous and Lady Diana commented that it had been "quite difficult" settling the guest list. Her flatmates sat in the front row. A notable absentee was her step-grandmother Barbara Cartland; it seemed a shame she was not there somehow. Instead, the formidable romantic novelist squeezed herself into an Order of St John uniform for the benefit of the television audience and proposed a toast to the couple wishing them "like us, a life of service". In a singular remark, the Dean of St Paul's had said that if he could share his seat with anyone to see the ceremony he would gladly do so. There certainly would not have been room on that seat for the 26-stone King of Tonga for whom a specially reinforced chair had to be installed.

The King, whose beaming mother stole the show at the Coronation in 1953, was one of a goodly number of foreign royalties attending the wedding – a gratifying turn-out in view of the fact that our Queen never attends specifically 'royal' events overseas. Missing from the procession of foreign crowned heads listed in the programme, though, were the King and Queen of Spain. Wretchedly, this admirable pair were obliged to pull out at the eleventh hour due to internal political pressure over the question of Gibraltar which featured on the itinerary of the planned wedding tour. The European royalties, who included the Princess of Monaco (the former Grace Kelly who did not repeat her *gaffe* at Princess Anne's wedding where she wore white) and her son, set out for St Paul's by car from Buckingham Palace shortly after various junior members of the Royal Family. Among the latter were the second wives of the Earl of Harewood and his brother Gerald Lascelles; both had had children out of wedlock (subsequently, of course, legitimised) and this was the first time they had been publicly welcomed into the fold, so to speak.

Next from the Palace, amidst the sort of cheers that always somehow exceed one's expectations, came the Queen's procession. The young Earl of Ulster, son of the Duke of Gloucester, leaning out of the fourth carriage to wave energetically to the packed spectators along the route was an especially memorable sight. The procession of the Prince of Wales followed; Prince Andrew, in his midshipman's uniform, travelled with the bridegroom, in Royal Navy No 1 day dress, in the 1902 State Landau. In keeping with royal traditions (and as predicted by the present writer in the *Spectator*), the bridegroom had decided to have two supporters, in the form of his brothers, rather than a best man.

The two Princes were greeted inside the Cathedral by the Archbishop of Canterbury in a specially made silver cope

that gave him the look of a refugee from *Dr Who*. The bridegroom's final bachelor wave to the world from the top of St Paul's steps brought a lump to many throats. After some horseplay over the ring from the strapping Prince Andrew, it was time to head down the aisle to the strains of Purcell's *Trumpet Tune*. Surrounded as he was by some seven men, the bridegroom's progress rather recalled a lamb being led to the slaughter, but the Prince managed a few surreptitious winks to friends and relations.

At five minutes to eleven, the bride's procession reached the steps of St Paul's which Lord Spencer gamely mounted, his chauffeur at his side. Now Lady Diana had arrived at the centre of the stage. The crushed dress bounced into shape; the train spread itself down the steps and then trailed dramatically behind her on the aisle. She looked sensational. It was noticeable that she had lost weight since the engagement and this leaner look in the face enhanced her beauty. Smiling, as she had been all the

way in the Glass Coach, and looking remarkably calm and assured, she seemed to guide her father down towards the altar as the *Trumpet Voluntary* blared out. "You look wonderful," said the Prince, at journey's end. "Wonderful for you," she replied – or so the lip readers would have us believe.

The bride did not promise to 'obey'; the Archbishop of Canterbury, Dr Robert Runcie, having made the old jest that it was "a bad thing to start your marriage off with a downright lie". She reversed the order of the Prince's names ("Philip Charles ...") in an attack of nerves with which everyone who has been married could sympathize; perhaps as a reciprocal gesture, the Prince made a hash of one of his responses ("All thy goods with thee I share"). Eagle-eyed royalty watchers picked up a "well done" from Prince Philip and an "it's all right" when no one decided to put his oar in at the pause for "any impediment". When the bride said "I will", the crowd outside, listening to a relay of the service, roared – as *The Times* said – "like a giant in approbation".

Other vignettes of the service linger in the memory: the Queen, in aquamarine, trying to control her laughter when an over-enthusiastic choirmaster knocked off a lampshade; the Queen Mother, in almond green and the familiar osprey plumes, dabbing away a tear and having to sit down at one stage – apparently not feeling her best. Then there was Princess Margaret crossing herself at the blessing and shaking her head at Lord Linley when the rest of the royal party moved off to sign the register. Surprisingly, the controversial issue of the royal surname, which the late Lord Mountbatten had hoped to see resolved on this occasion with 'Mountbatten-Windsor' being entered in the register (as it had been at Princess Anne's wedding), was unaffected by the bridegroom's description with only his royal styles and no surname. Mrs Shand Kydd took her former husband's arm on the way to the Dean's aisle.

During these formalities backstage, Kiri Te Kanawa, the Maori opera star, looking like some exotic bird of paradise in a somewhat unfortunate hat, crossed herself and gave a divine rendition of the Seraphim aria from Handel's *Samson*. The Prince and Princess's hopes for a musical wedding were fabulously fulfilled. The anthems and the performances of Miss Te Kanawa and the Bach Choir were quite unforgettable. Especially moving was the Princess's favourite hymn since schooldays, *I Vow to Thee My Country* which is seldom heard these

days thanks to trendily unpatriotic parsons. Perhaps out of consideration for the various statesmen in the congregation the verse of the National Anthem including the couplet "Frustrate their knavish tricks/Confound their politicks" was omitted. For the procession of the bride and the bridegroom on the way out, the Cathedral was awash with Elgar's *Pomp and Circumstance*.

The pomp of the Queen's procession, though, was toned down to enable Her Majesty to walk with Lord Spencer and the Duke of Edinburgh with Mrs Shand Kydd – a break with precedent. Her Royal Highness The Princess of Wales

(as she had now become) had lifted her veil – reminding everybody how young she was – and curtsied to the Queen before making her exit on the arm of her new husband.

The bells rang out as they came through the West Door to receive the ecstatic greetings of the multitude. The cheers echoed all along the route back to the Palace as the Prince and Princess responded warmly from the 1902 State Landau, an open carriage that gave even the most incompetent photographer a chance. The crowds surged down the Mall in readiness for the balcony appearances, showing that a mass of humanity need not always be an alarming or disorderly mob. And then, at ten minutes past one, out came the members of the wedding, through the glass doors on to the balcony to acknowledge a blast of sound from an ocean of happy faces as far as the eye could see. Egged on by Prince Andrew, the Prince of Wales eventually consented to repeat the kiss he had given his bride in the surprisingly small Centre Room within. (The lip readers claim the bridegroom's initial reaction was that he was not "going in for that sort of caper".)

Following the wedding breakfast, which centred around *suprême de volaille Princesse de Galles*, in the Ball Supper Room, the Princess herself changed into a fetching apricot number designed by Belville Sassoon for the 'going away'. Hereabouts the hitherto immaculate timing went astray and commentators (such as the present writer on independent radio) found themselves having to fill in with recondite details of the history of Waterloo Station, Broadlands, or the presence of the Prince's friend Colonel Andrew Parker Bowles in the departure detachment. However, at 4.20, the Prince and Princess emerged from the inner quadrangle, duly showered by rose petals and confetti. 'Just Married' was scrawled on a placard at the back of the open landau and an especially nice touch was the bunch of balloons billowing up behind the postillions. Somehow these cheerful blue and silver balloons seemed to symbolize that, for all the splendour and pageantry, it was ultimately very much a young people's day.

In a characteristically spontaneous and human gesture, the Princess thanked the owlish master of ceremonies, Lord Maclean, the Lord Chamberlain, and his henchman Sir 'Johnny' Johnston, with a kiss each at Waterloo before boarding the train to Broadlands. The last time the engine driver had driven a special train in that direction was to convey the coffin of Lord Mountbatten, whose absence on this wedding day was doubtless a cause of special sadness for the Prince. But Broadlands was the place where his parents had begun their honeymoon in 1947 and the Prince has a strong feeling for tradition.

The Prince and Princess were still waving from the window of their carriage as the train pulled out of the station. From Romsey to the gates of Broadlands the route was again lined with flag-waving crowds. It had been such a magical day that no one wanted it to end.

Opposite: The group picture at the Palace by Patrick Lichfield
Below: Westminster Bridge. Earth has not anything to show more fair

Princess of Wales

"O God, you who are the giver of all happiness because you are the giver of all love, we thank you and praise your name for the love you have given to these your servants, Charles, Prince of Wales and Diana, Princess of Wales," intoned the Reverend Harry Williams in St Paul's. To this former Dean of Trinity College, Cambridge, fell the honour of being the first to refer to the former Lady Diana Spencer in these terms. She had become the ninth holder of the title.

Although there have been some twenty Princes of Wales since 1301 when the future Edward II was given the title, by a quirk of history only eight of them married while they were thus styled. The first Princess of Wales, Joan, Countess of Kent, never became Queen, as her husband the 'Black Prince', died in the lifetime of his father Edward III. Similarly, the son of Henry VI predeceased his father leaving his widow (the former Ann Nevill, daughter of the 'Kingmaker' Earl of Warwick) as Princess of Wales. Then there was Catherine of Aragon who first married Arthur, Prince of Wales, the eldest son of Henry VII; following Arthur's death (yet again in the lifetime of his father), she married the new Prince of Wales, later Henry VIII.

The day after the wedding of the new Princess of Wales, her marital coat-of-arms was issued by royal warrant. This entitled the Princess to bear and use her paternal arms of Spencer ('*Quarterly, argent and gules, in the second and third quarters a fret or, over all on a bend sable, three escallops of the first'*, in heraldic language) within a shield and impaled by the arms of the Prince. The shield was ensigned with the Prince's coronet and supported by a lion and a griffin. The latter, or sinister, supporter was something of an armorial innovation (being based on Lord Spencer's dexter supporter) and the Princess's use of her own family motto (*'Dieu defend le droit'*), rather than her spouse's, was also novel. The motto *'Ich Dien'*, though, and the familiar ostrich feathers featured on the joint armorial bearings approved early in 1982; this was a straightforward marshalling of the Prince's arms and the Spencer arms.

The Palace also made it clear that Her Royal Highness was not to be known as 'Princess Diana', but simply as 'The Princess of Wales' – or, perhaps at a pinch, 'The Princess Charles'. (To those who find the latter appellation strange, one might ask what is odd about being called 'Mrs John Smith' rather than 'Mrs Susan Smith'?) On the other hand, the Royal Family have made such a nonsense of these matters ('Mrs Mark Phillips' and 'the Honourable Mrs Angus Ogilvy', forsooth!), that one cannot be sure as to what might happen. The Dowager Duchess of Gloucester, for instance, is known as 'Princess Alice' rather than 'Princess Henry', following the precedent of the late Dowager Duchess of Kent being styled 'Princess Marina' rather than 'Princess George'. It can, of course, be argued that Princess Marina was already a Princess (of Greece and Denmark) in her own right, whereas Princess Alice (formerly Lady Alice Montagu-Douglas-Scott) was merely the daughter of a Duke. A pedant, though, might try to claim that 'Lady' as a prefix used to be synonymous with 'Princess' anyway and that thus the former Lady Diana could be styled 'Princess Diana'. It has even been suggested that Lady Diana was already a princess in her own right through her descent from the great Duke of Marlborough, Prince of Mindelheim (in Swabia) – a highly question-

Opposite: The honeymooners arrive at the 'Rock'
Below: On the bridge of Britannia

Below: The Royal Yacht and attendant vessels sail off
at the start of the honeymoon
Opposite top: A passage to Port Said
Opposite below: The Princess steps ashore in Egypt
(left) and, accompanied by Mrs Sadat, leaves
Hurghada airport on the way home (right)

able proposition. Whatever the ins and outs of it all, there seems little way of stopping her from being widely referred to as 'Princess Diana' or, for that matter, 'Princess Di'.

That was what she was being called, of course, in the popular newspapers as they followed the itinerary of the wedding tour. After three nights at Broadlands – temporarily vacated by Lord and Lady Romsey, to whose son, Nicholas, the Princess was to become godmother – the Prince and Princess flew to the problematical port of Gibraltar where they embarked on the Royal Yacht, *Britannia*,

for a cruise away from it all around the Greek islands in the Mediterranean. It was a chance, at long last, to relax in glorious weather and even more glorious privacy.

They sailed back into the limelight twelve days later at Port Said, where they were joined for dinner on board by Egypt's President, the courageous Anwar Sadat and his wife Jihan. The President awarded the Prince the Order of the Republic of Egypt, first class. Poignantly, he was to wear it all too soon at the President's funeral after the statesman had been gunned down. For,

apart from the royal wedding, it was a year of disturbing violence. But that warm summer night was a pleasant and memorable one for the Prince and Princess: "something like a family occasion", as the British Ambassador observed. Before flying to Scotland at the end of their honeymoon cruise, they said goodbye to the Sadats at the Hurghada airfield and, in another of her charmingly natural gestures, the Princess blew the President and his wife a kiss before boarding the aircraft.

The couple had been remarkably successful at eluding the press as they weaved their way through the Greek islands and the Prince sent messages of thanks to the Greek government for their assistance in this direction. The Prime Minister, however, had turned down an invitation to dine on *Britannia*, which some tried to blow up into a 'snub'. Back at Balmoral, the circus of professional royalty watchers assembled once more, though the honeymoon was still in progress. Facing the cameras again, the Princess talked happily to the attendant hacks. The cruise had been "fabulous". She highly recommended married life and said that Balmoral was the best place in the world. Asking whether a pressman's bouquet had gone on expenses, though, was a less endearing remark. Short of copy, apart from the usual sorties to Crathie church, the Braemar gathering (where the Princess was introduced to the crowd as the

"Duchess of Rothesay", the heir apparent being traditionally called by this Dukedom in Scotland) and so forth, the press resorted to inventing stuff. The Princess was said to be wretched, withdrawn, lonely and a worry to the Queen.

Meanwhile in London, the Princess's controversial betrousered portrait by Bryan Organ was slashed in the National Portrait Gallery by a young man from Belfast, who went to prison for his pains. The press were able to make a meal of this and managed to drum up something

Opposite: Some of the wedding presents on show at St James's Palace
Below left: The Duke and Duchess of Rothesay back on Scottish soil
Right: The honeymooners at Balmoral

in Scotland; there were allegations that the animal-loving Princess had shot and wounded a stag while deer-stalking. This developed into a right royal rumpus with the Buckingham Palace press office duly issuing another denial. Perhaps the honeymoon was going on rather too long. Save for the odd trip down to Highgrove to chase up the slow progress in the work at her new home – the Princess was said to be in tears because the builders were behind schedule – or the visit to the exhibition of her wedding presents at St James's Palace (which, together with the wedding souvenirs, raised some £750,000 for handicapped charities), the Princess continued her Scottish sojourn into the autumn. Eventually the 'silly season' came to an end and the media were able to devote their attentions to covering the three-day tour of Wales.

It was no less than a triumph for the Princess. Her husband put the overwhelming success of their visit to the Principality down to the "effect that my

dear wife has on everybody". Everywhere she went on the exhausting 400-mile trek through Wales the crowds came to see her and they were not disappointed. "Now I've seen her, she's everything I thought she would be," said one woman at Rhydyfelin. "She's the flower in the royal forest." Veteran royalty watchers considered that the Princess's natural charm and ability to put overawed gawpers at ease outdistanced the rest of the Royal Family – even such popular figures as the Queen Mother and Princess Alexandra. The Prince of Wales defined his role on the tour as "just a collector of flowers" and regretted that he hadn't "got enough wives to go round". Whether joking with children at Llanelwedd – clamping her hand across her mouth in girlish glee – or chatting up pensioners ("What nice shiny medals") at the Deeside Leisure Centre near Shotton, the Princess always struck the right note. Maintain-

ing her reputation for spontaneous kissing, she gave Lord Snowdon a peck at Caernarvon, when the Prince revisited the scene of his investiture. Although he is the best Prince of Wales the Welsh have ever had, a lunatic fringe of nationalists were intent on causing some trouble during the tour but only partially succeeded; just the odd scuffle breaking out. One placard read 'Go home English Princess', though (as we saw in Chapter Three) in fact she has plenty of Welsh blood and is descended from Owen Glendower himself, the last 'native' Prince of Wales.

She even managed a few words of Welsh in her speech of thanks to the City Council of Cardiff when she was awarded the freedom of the city. "How proud I am to be Princess of such a wonderful place, and of the Welsh, who are very special to me," she said in a

Below: The Princess in her element at the maternity ward of Llwynypia Hospital
Opposite left: On the steps of the throne: the Princess at her first State Opening of Parliament
Right: The fashion leader at the première of
For Your Eyes Only

touching little speech. Comparisons with the young Duchess of York (now the Queen Mother) were the best anyone could do to find a precedent for this infusion of youth, beauty, charm and, above all, cheerfulness into the Royal Family. Earlier in the day, the Prince and Princess had visited a maternity ward, causing speculation as to her pregnancy. ''The Princess just came into our ward and said: 'Oh babies', before rushing over to see our children,'' reported Wendy Nash from the Rhondda. ''She asked lots of questions about labour and peeped into the cot to see my baby boy. It was obvious she absolutely loved children.'' The Prince was also showing a lively interest; he opined that it was a very good thing for a husband to be present at the birth.

The speculation was soon to be confirmed, but the Princess initially carried

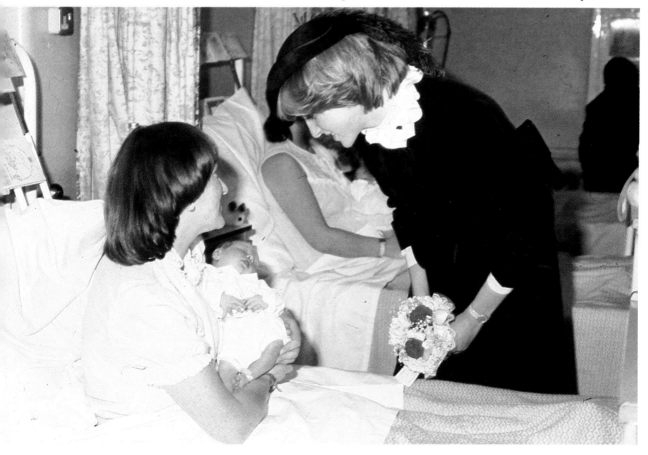

on with a heavy programme of engagements. Her stylish clothes created quite a stir in the fashion world and it was clear that she was the mistress of her own wardrobe. The key names, according to Suzy Menkes of *The Times*, were Caroline Charles (whose designs for the Princess included the tartan suit for the Braemar Games and the cream cashmere coat and skirt seen in Wales and at Balmoral); Donald Campbell (whose red and green suit was so appropriate for Wales); Bellville Sassoon (whose chief commission had been the going-away outfit) and milliner John Boyd, who has also made hats for Mrs Shand Kydd and Mrs Thatcher. The Princess's country clothes tend to come from Bill Pashley of Battersea. He prefers her "in sporty outdoor clothes and with her hair all windblown". In formal dress Pashley feels "she tends to freeze". Some useful tips came from *Vogue*, where the other Spencer girls had worked; the Princess has certainly given the fashion writers plenty of copy.

Virtually every day there seemed to be a photograph of the Princess in the newspapers wearing some striking new ensemble. On Sunday 1 November, for instance, having moved into Highgrove that weekend, the Princess attended the christening of her godson, Nicholas Knatchbull, at Romsey and in the evening went to her ancestral home of Blenheim Palace for a concert given by the English Chamber Orchestra; on Monday, she went to the opening of the London Film Festival at the National Film Theatre and on Wednesday she made her first appearance at the State Opening of Parliament (shimmering in a bridal white gown of chiffon by Bellville Sassoon and wearing a diamond tiara, but with her hair still down rather than up). That evening she went to the gala

opening of the *Splendours of the Gonzaga* exhibition at the Victoria & Albert Museum – whose director, Roy Strong (now Sir Roy), in a memorable slip referred to these treasures from "Manchester . . . I mean Mantua" – and the Prince was heard to say that they had "had a lot of culture this week". On the Thursday the Prince and Princess lunched with the Lord Mayor at the Guildhall – an event which took on an extra special significance since it had been announced that morning that the Princess was indeed expecting a baby the following June.

The announcement from the Palace stated that the Princess was in "excellent health" and that she hoped "to continue to undertake some public engagements but regrets any disappointment which may be caused by any curtailment of her planned programme". What this meant, naturally, was that Her Royal Highness would be unable to make the proposed visits to Australia, New Zealand and Canada in 1982. Although the news of the Princess's pregnancy was received amid general euphoria, some grousers thought that such a full programme should not have been planned in the circumstances anyway and that the Princess should have waited before starting a family. (One wonders what people would have to talk about if the Royal Family didn't exist.) A mass of recondite gynaecological and genealogical material was presented for the edification of the public – such as the fact that it was the quickest royal pregnancy since Alexandra, Princess of Wales, produced the unfortunate Duke of Clarence in January 1864, just ten months after her marriage.

Inevitably, the Princess's morning sickness and the other side effects of pregnancy led to cancellations of engagements, causing unavoidable disappointment. A visit to the Duchy of Cornwall estates in the West Country had to be called off, a trip to Bristol and so on. "No one told me I would feel like I did," the Princess confided to a bystander on a tour of the north. A York schoolgirl asked the Princess if she wanted a boy or a girl. "I don't mind as long as it is healthy," was the reply. A morris dancer in Chesterfield waved a pig's bladder on a stick at the Prince and told him that this fertility symbol might signify twins. "You can keep the bloody thing," said the Prince. Interestingly enough, although there have never been twins in the history of the Royal Family, the Princess's pedigree reveals that both her maternal grandfather, the fourth Lord Fermoy, and his wife's father, Colonel William Gill, were twins; experts say that twins on the mother's side can be especially significant.

The pregnant Princess plugged on gamely, though showing signs of strain. She assured well-wishers that she felt fine when she fulfilled her first solo public engagement by switching on the Regent Street Christmas lights on 18 November in the driving rain. Her second solo effort was opening the Post Office administrative centre at Northampton, near the Spencer seat of Althorp where she lunched beforehand with her father and step-mother. The great treasure-house was now staying open through the winter to meet the popular demand. At the beginning of December the Prince and Princess dined with the Speaker of the House of Commons, George Thomas, who had read the lesson at their wedding in his lilting Welsh voice; but, to the particular displeasure of the Prime Minister, the evening was interrupted by the division bells following a demonstration by Tam Dalyell, the unpredictable socialist laird.

The constant scrutiny of the Princess's every move by the media was taking its toll on this vulnerable twenty-year-old and there was increasing concern among the Royal Family about her health. After the sensational tabloids had splashed pictures of the Princess shopping in Tetbury and kissing the Prince at Highgrove – which is situated conveniently close to the road for operators of telephoto lenses – the Queen and the Palace press office decided to try to stop the rot and make Fleet Street see reason. The editors of Britain's national newspapers – with the exception of the editor of the *Sun* – and various television and radio executives assembled for a briefing.

The Queen's press secretary, Michael Shea, told them that the media's obsession with the Princess of Wales – which was just as strong among such papers as *The Times* and the *Daily Telegraph* as it was with, say, the *Daily Mirror* – was

Opposite: The Princess at the gala opening of the Splendours of the Gonzaga *exhibition at the Victoria & Albert Museum*

beginning to produce alarming signs of strain in the Princess, who had a feeling of media claustrophobia. The editors discussed the matter over drinks with the Queen, whose attitude was more that of an anxious mother-in-law than an outraged monarch. The clear impression was gained that Her Majesty had formed a deep bond of affection and understanding with her new daughter-in-law and that she did not want to force the Princess to change her nature so as to conform to royal tradition. It appeared that the Royal Family's view was that the Princess, having been brought up to freedom and independence, could not possibly be expected to surrender totally that side of her character. Thus, significantly, there were pointers to a new and less hidebound style of life for the next generation of royalty.

The beleaguered Princess felt that she was being denied the personal freedoms necessary to her at such a time of her life and it was especially interesting that the Queen herself did not seem to be going along with the traditional view that personal restrictions have to go hand in hand with royal duties. Obviously Her Majesty believed that the Princess, as a unique addition to the Royal Family, should be allowed to create a new pattern of royal existence, which might well include informal and private excursions in the public eye when off duty. For instance, if the Princess had a sudden craving for wine gums, why shouldn't she feel free to go down to the local village shop to buy some without being confronted by photographers reversing down the pavement? The editor of the *News of the World's* observed at the meeting that a servant could buy the wine gums on her behalf. The Queen apparently retorted that that was one of the more pompous remarks that she had heard. (The gentleman concerned left the editorial chair not long afterwards, incidentally.)

The Prince of Wales, said to be particularly upset, even angry, about the invasion of his wife's privacy, was not present at the meeting. It was made clear that the Princess was determined to carry out as many public engagements as possible – coverage of which she accepted and welcomed – before her confinement. And this she duly did. Thankfully the intrusiveness decreased.

One of the Princess's last scheduled engagements before disappearing from public view in readiness for the birth was to be at the Sony factory at Bridgend, Glamorgan, on 7 April. The creation of several thousand jobs here in an area of acute unemployment was largely thanks to the Prince of Wales's meeting the Sony chairman in Tokyo. (Who says that the Prince does nothing for Wales?)

As the Princess prepared for the arrival of her baby, she had the satisfaction of knowing that, according to a survey, she had become the nation's favourite royal person.

A Great Challenge

On 1 July 1982 the Princess of Wales celebrates her 21st birthday; an event suitably marked by special stamps. Ahead lies a daunting prospect of duty as she tackles the roles of wife, mother, royal personage in her own right, consort and Queen. "My life will be a great challenge," she said before her wedding. But she felt her age gave her "a good start" and that "interests will broaden as my life goes on".

Any attempt at an assessment of her character at the age of 21 is bound to be premature. Already she has come on tremendously from the girl of nineteen with endearingly awkward mannerisms. The impersonators who specialise in her tilting chin and sideways glances need to get a new act together. That shy vulnerability, which has contributed to her artless charm and immense appeal, is becoming less evident. As one school-friend said: "She's reserved rather than shy. She's got her own ideas, and she isn't easily swayed by what people say. She's got a lot of go in her." Her former flatmate Virginia Pitman is convinced she will "carry it off", describing her as "a tremendous fighter". There is little doubt that, for all the upsets and anxieties, she is tougher than she looks. And she will need to be.

Some saw evidence of this in the swift departure of the Prince of Wales's manservant, an incident which bore out Jeeves's experience that 'when the wife comes in at the front door the valet of bachelor days goes out at the back'. She has been hurrying along the redecoration of Highgrove and has installed a Welsh solicitor's daughter as cook-housekeeper. Inevitably, in what Carolyn Pride described as "her new world", the Princess has been cut off from almost all her old friends. "For heaven's sake ring me up," she told one upon her engagement, "I'm going to need you". But one could say that in every marriage the wife's girl-friends are drastically pruned. A particular interest for the royalty watchers will be the formation of her own court circle.

With due respect to Anne Beckwith-Smith, Lavinia Baring and Hazel Alston-Roberts-West, doubtless all estimable and worthy persons, the Princess would seem to have been saddled with three ladies-in-waiting who are not only all in their thirties – Mrs West is 38 in May 1982 – but appear to possess the horsey hallmarks of the traditional royal household. If, as the Queen apparently implied to the Fleet Street editors, we are going to see a less stuffy pattern of royal life established by the young Princess, it is to be hoped that, in due course and once she has learnt the ropes, she will be able to gather some supporters from among her own generation to help her with her duties.

"Well, obviously it's children," said the former kindergarten assistant when asked what her main interests in the royal round will be. When asked about their schedule of engagements before the marriage, the Prince of Wales pointed out that "quite a lot will be joint, obviously, and certainly to begin with". The Princess has so far acquired little experience of travelling abroad, though travel is something she enjoys, and the Prince added that he thought "obviously when we go abroad they will be joint". But, as the Prince observed from his own experience of embarking on full-scale

Opposite left: 'Over to you': the Princess hands a present for her baby to lady-in-waiting, Anne Beckwith-Smith
Opposite right: The Princess with another of her ladies-in-waiting, Lavinia Baring
Below: The practised hand with children at the Guildford Cathedral carol service

royal life in his early twenties: "I think that as Diana begins to do various things or get involved in the children's things, that very often you get many more invitations, you meet more people, you suddenly find areas or things that you think 'My goodness I must . . . I'd like to do something about improving things here or encouraging there.' And after a bit you develop your own sphere."

The first batch of the Princess's new patronages and presidencies was announced in February 1982. From the 150 or so organizations that had called for her services, Her Royal Highness's initial choice settled upon the Royal School for the Blind, the Welsh National Opera, the Malcolm Sargent Cancer Fund for Children, the Pre-School Playgroups Association and the Albany, a community centre in South-East London that deals with children at risk.

On the subject of the Prince and Princess of Wales's household it is worth stressing the point that they and their staff do not cost the public a penny. They live on the income of the Prince's own revenues from the Duchy of Cornwall which is, of course, very considerable (over half-a-million pounds a year) and the Prince does not pay income tax. However, when he became entitled to the Duchy income at the age of 21, the Prince offered half, subject to review, to the Consolidated Fund administered by the Exchequer. Faced with rising running expenses after his marriage, the Prince has now revised this to a quarter.

For, as the Princess pointed out on the subject of wedding presents, they have "two houses to fill". In the wake of what *The Times* aptly described as "the indecisive muddle over Chevening", that fine Palladian seat of the Stanhopes near Sevenoaks (and West Heath, the Princess's old school) which the Prince

never really liked, the Duchy of Cornwall bought Highgrove, a considerably inferior country house in the Royal Family's beloved 'Beaufortshire', in 1980. There is now a remarkable 'royal triangle' in this corner of the Cotswolds, with the Highgrove estate of some 348 acres being set only a few miles apart from those of Princess Anne and Captain Mark Phillips at Gatcombe – saved, incidentally, from becoming a lunatic asylum in the 1940s by 'Rab' Butler's father-in-law – and Prince and Princess Michael of Kent at Nether Lypiatt. Highgrove certainly lacks the architectural charm of Nether Lypiatt and is a surprisingly modest residence for the heir to the throne.

In his *Delineations of Gloucestershire (1825–27)*, though, J N Brewer observed that it was "well suited to the domestic and hospitable purposes of a family of high respectability". Built in the late 1790s by John Paul Paul, it is a rectangular three-storey block of five by three bays, with pilasters. The house was severely damaged by fire in 1893 and nearly £6000 was spent on its restoration the following year. A nineteenth-century domestic wing was demolished in 1966 and elegant eighteenth-century fireplaces have been introduced from elsewhere. The garden side has bay windows which probably date from after the fire. The original lodge of 1798 – as we have seen, it is irritatingly close to the public road – survives with rusticated gates; though the latter are being replaced by a new pair as a wedding present to Their Royal Highnesses from the town of Tetbury. This handsome gesture was initiated by the mayor after the Prince had expressed his admiration for the gates outside Tetbury churchyard.

The church contains several memorials to the Paul family who built High-

grove. They were prosperous clothiers of Huguenot descent who settled in Tetbury in the eighteenth century. One branch of the family, the Dean Pauls, included a baronet who married a granddaughter of the eighth Earl of Strathmore (an ancestor of the Queen Mother). Unfortunately, their son was deported to Australia for fraud and another member of the family to achieve notoriety was that tragic figure, Brenda Dean Paul, dubbed 'the society drug addict' in the gossip columns in which she featured so frequently up until her death in 1959. The Pauls sold Highgrove in 1860; subsequent families associated with the place have included those of Strachey, Yatman, Mitchell (who rebuilt the house after the fire) and Morgan-Jones. In 1974 Highgrove was purchased by Harold Macmillan's son, Maurice, who sold it to the Duchy of Cornwall.

The Princess is said to have told friends: "It's perfect. I couldn't wish for a nicer house." The decorative work is being supervised by Dudley Poplak,

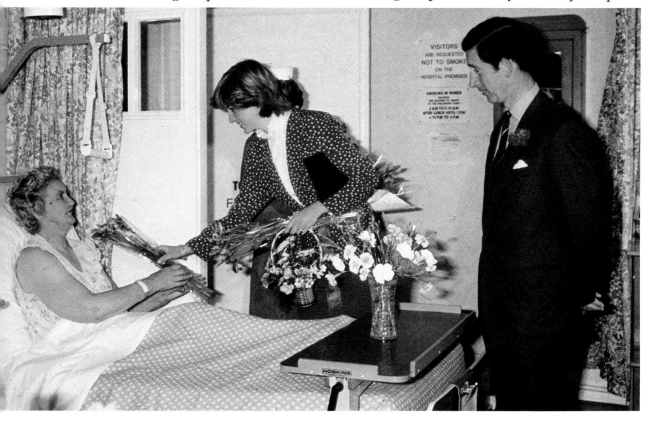

who apparently replaced Lord Mount-batten's son-in-law, David Hicks in the job; as indeed he also did at Gatcombe. Their Royal Highnesses also have a bun-galoid bolt-hole in the Scilly Islands and it has been predicted that the Queen will give them a retreat on the Balmoral estate with the rather unfortunate name of Delnadamph Lodge. A Welsh home would seem to be a popular move for the future.

The first London residence of the Prince and Princess will comprise some newly renovated apartments in what is known in royal circles as 'the Aunt Heap', Kensington Palace. The building we see today, elegant and comfortable in its warm red brick, is largely the work of Sir Christopher Wren who, with Nicholas Hawksmoor as his clerk, rebuilt Nottingham House (as it was originally called) after it had been bought by William III in 1689. The asthmatic King wanted somewhere away from the fumes of Whitehall and his three succes-sors on the throne all preferred Kensington, later done over by William Kent, to their other palaces. It was deserted after George II's death, but came back into prominence as the childhood home of Queen Victoria. Queen Mary also spent part of her childhood here and considered making Kensington Palace the London residence of herself and King George V in preference to Buckingham Palace. Several other members of the present Royal Family have apartments in the 'Court Suburb' and its oldest ever member, Princess Alice, Countess of Athlone, died here in 1981.

The Princess said before her wedding that she was "looking forward to being a good wife" and the Prince was already finding it "marvellous to have a lot of support". There is, of course, a disparity in their ages of a dozen years but their senses of humour – ranging from *The Goons* to Miss Piggy of *The Muppets* and *Not the Nine o'Clock News* – should bridge the gap. Music is an important bond and, even if the Princess is certainly not horsey by royal standards, they both like the fresh air and the country. The Prince is a curiously enigmatic figure whose personality blends a somewhat distressing service heartiness with a basic sensitivity; a thirst for the chase with a feeling for the arts; maturity with a residual boyishness and broad humour with a deep seriousness and a sense of history. Although, as Philip Howard observed in *The Times*, "the older Hooray Henrys . . . seem to the captious to be too numerous among his close friends", it is well to remember that at his right hand he has an outstandingly able and wise private secretary, Edward Adeane, who comes from a veritable dynasty of royal courtiers. The *Tatler* has predicted that the Prince and Princess could make traditional values fashionable again: "Healthy, happy and hearty, the Prince and Princess of Wales will be the new leaders of the straight."

The Prince is ready for family life and, as he has said, the Princess will keep him young. They need time to settle down and make their own life together. This is

one of the reasons why any chance of the Queen abdicating seems remote; she wants to give them a period of relatively carefree family life denied her and the Duke of Edinburgh by her father's tragically early death. But the Queen's sense of duty would also militate against any idea of stepping down. As the Prince of Wales himself has pointed out, the longer that she is on the throne the better a sovereign she becomes. The advantages to the country of having a monarch who can take a long view of things cannot be emphasized too strongly. ("No, Mr Banneman," said Queen Victoria to her Secretary of State for War in the 1890s, "Lord Palmerston proposed exactly the same thing to me in '52 and Lord Palmerston was wrong.") Already in her 30 years as Queen, Elizabeth II has seen eight prime ministers; she has acquired considerable political experience that will stand her in good stead when faced with the constitutional crisis of a 'hung' Parliament which only she has the power to untangle. The point is that the monarchy is an hereditary office, not just a job, and it is difficult to imagine

the Queen retiring. Perhaps, in the Queen's very old age, Prince Charles might become Prince Regent and as time goes by it is to be hoped that he will be brought increasingly into state affairs through the Privy Council and so forth.

There is plenty of time for all that later on. For the moment, the Princess of Wales will, of course, be preoccupied with her role as a mother. Former colleagues at the Young England Kindergarten are in no doubt that she will make an excellent one; her style of motherhood will surely set new standards. The infant Prince or Princess – or twins, if you took advantage of the odds of 15 to 1 against offered by William Hill – will become second in line to the throne. The baby will be known as 'His Royal Highness Prince (christian name) of Wales' or 'Her Royal Highness Princess (christian name) of Wales'. Having regard to the Princess's own royal ancestry, one might expect 'James' and 'Henry' to be among the boys' names to be considered, though 'George' seems a safer bet and 'Louis' (after Lord Mountbatten) can be backed for a place. The Princess's father's name, John, is regarded as unlucky – the last child to be born to a Prince and Princess of Wales was the epileptic Prince John (1905–19) – and her own brother, John, died as a baby. The choice of names for a girl is wider, for she is less likely to become sovereign – being replaced as heir by any subsequent male child – and presumably includes Elizabeth and Frances, and perhaps Victoria. It is interesting to note that, thanks to the Princess, the Prince's eventual successor on the throne will be the most 'British' sovereign since the Stuarts with some 58.8 per cent British blood (and 4.69 American).

'God bless the Princess of Wales too' has already been added to the words of that fine Welsh anthem – and deservedly so. One prays that Her Royal Highness will not become spoilt on the one hand, or bored on the other; but there is no reason to suppose that she will. As one of her former flatmates said, the Prince of Wales is "very lucky to have got her". So are her adulatory future subjects.

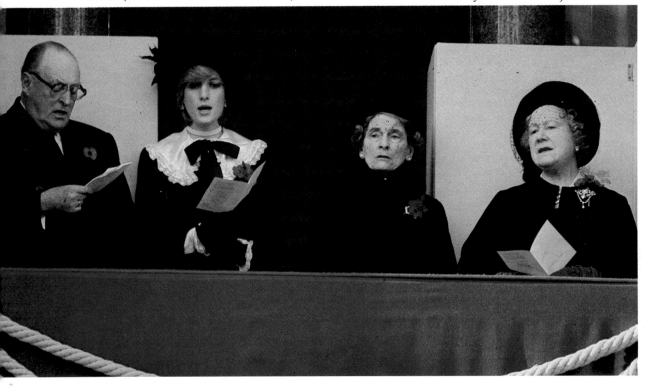

*Opposite: The Princess with the Queen Mother,
Princess Alice and the King of Norway at the
Remembrance Day ceremony in Whitehall
Below: To the manner born, she puts a small boy at
his ease in Hyde Park during a tree-planting
ceremony*

Acknowledgements

Antler Books and the author gratefully
acknowledge the assistance of the following in
the production of this book: Susan Abbott,
Camilla Darell, Helen Fraser, Charles Kidd,
Caroline Lort-Phillips, Lucinda McNeile, Patrick
Mortemore, Michael Sayer, Denis Strange, Nick
Thornton, Hugo Vickers, Tom Williams, David
Williamson

Picture Acknowledgements

Most of the pictures in this book have been
supplied by Tim Graham. Others have been
supplied as follows:
Associated Newspapers, *35*
Beedle and Cooper, *25*
Camera Press, *28, 29 (bottom left), 29 (top right),
39 (bottom right), 66*
Central Press, *45*
Fox Photos, *29 (centre), 49, 79 (left), 87*
Margaret Gill, *23*
Anwar Hussein, *68*
Keystone Press, *17 (left), 84*
Margaret Lavender, *88*
Mike Lloyd, *51, 53*
London News Service, *74*
Mansell Collection, *27*
Photo Library, *33 (bottom), 57, 59, 63, 65, 67*
Press Association, *4, 33 (top), 34, 43 (right), 50,
56 (left), 92*
Mike Roberts, *47 (right)*
John Scott, *12, 26, 93*
Syndication International, *29 (bottom right), 52,
61, 75, 78*
UPP, *17 (right)*